W9-DES-539

I'M AN AMERICAN CITIZEN

The Many People of America

Joanna Anderson

New York

Published in 2013 by The Rosen Publishing Group, Inc.
29 East 21st Street, New York, NY 10010

Book Design: Michael Harmon

Photo Credits: Cover © iStockphoto.com/Photomorphic; p. 4 Jupiterimages/Thinkstock.com; pp. 5, 6 Digital Vision./Thinkstock.com; p. 7 (book) SergiyN/Shutterstock.com; p. 7 (soccer) Digital Media Pro/Shutterstock.com; p. 8 Jose Luis Pelaez Inc/Blend Images/Getty Images; pp. 9, 16 iStockphoto/Thinkstock.com; pp. 10, 11, 22 Hemera/Thinkstock.com; p. 12 Dick Luria/Thinkstock.com; p. 13 Lisa S./Shutterstock.com; p. 14 (tacos) Julenochek/Shutterstock.com; p. 14 (sushi) White78/Shutterstock.com; p. 14 (thai food) Dzinnik/Shutterstock.com; p. 14 (samosa) highviews/Shutterstock.com; p. 15 Jack Hollingsworth/Thinkstock.com; p. 18 © iStockphoto.com/CEFutcher; p. 19 aceshot1/Shutterstock.com; p. 20 Golden Pixels LLC/Shutterstock.com; p. 21 R. Gino Santa Maria/Shutterstock.com.

Library of Congress Cataloging-in-Publication Data

Anderson, Joanna, 1980-
The many people of America / Joanna Anderson.
p. cm. — (I'm an American citizen)
Includes bibliographical references and index.
ISBN: 978-1-4488-8866-5
6-pack ISBN: 978-1-4488-8867-2
ISBN: 978-1-4488-8591-6 (library binding)
1. United States—Population—Juvenile literature. 2. Multiculturalism—United States—Juvenile literature. 3. Ethnology—United States—Juvenile literature. I. Title.
E184.A1A6728 2013
305.800973—dc23

2012014001

Manufactured in the United States of America

CPSIA Compliance Information: Batch #WS12RC: For further information contact Rosen Publishing, New York, New York at 1-800-237-9932.

Word Count: 465

Contents

Diversity

Many people live in the United States. Our country is special because we believe all people have the right to be different.

Our differences are called **diversity**. Diversity means there are many kinds of things. Being different is a good thing. It makes our country interesting!

One place we see diversity is in school. There are boys and girls in your class. Your classmates have different skin colors. They have different hair and eye colors, too.

Sometimes, the things we do make us different. Some of your friends might like to read, while others like to play sports. These differences make us special.

What Makes Us Different?

Many people are born in the United States. Some Americans move here from other countries. This is one thing that makes us all different.

A long time ago, people moved to America because their countries didn't want them to be different. America was a safe place for them to be happy and free.

As more people moved to America, it became more diverse. Americans started to look different. Today, there are black Americans and white Americans.

There are **Hispanic** Americans and **Asian** Americans. There are **Native Americans** and many other kinds of people, too. We're different, but we're all Americans.

Showing Our Differences

When people came to America, they brought the best parts of their old home with them. These things became part of American life.

Today, we cook special food, wear **traditional** clothing, and share certain beliefs to honor our past. Learning about them helps us understand differences.

One way to learn about different kinds of people is by trying their special food. There are a few ways to try different foods. You can buy some food at the store.

You can also try cooking at home with your family. Your mom or dad may know some foods that your family ate long ago. It's fun to try new things!

Trying new foods is a great way to learn about different people. You may have already eaten foods from other countries! Can you think of some?

Foods from Around the World

People who have come from other countries have different clothes, too. We can see our differences by looking at what people wear. It would be dull if we all dressed alike!

Sometimes, people wear traditional clothes. They wear them on holidays or simply when they want to. This is a great way to show we're different!

Another way to find out about other people is to learn about their beliefs. A belief is something you think is true.

In America, we have the right to believe in whatever we want. That's why so many people like living in our country.

America is a big country with many kinds of people. Learning about our differences shows that we respect other people. It's one way to be a good American!

Glossary

Asian (AY-zhuhn) Someone who comes from Asia or whose family comes from Asia.

diversity (duh-VUHR-suh-tee) When many things are different.

Hispanic (hih-SPA-nihk) Someone who comes from Latin America or whose family comes from Latin America.

Native American (NAY-tihv uh-MEHR-uh-kuhn) Someone who belongs to one of the first groups of people who lived in North America.

traditional (truh-DIH-shuh-nuhl) Having to do with something from the past that has been used for a long time.

Due to the changing nature of Internet links, The Rosen Publishing Group, Inc., has developed an online list of websites related to the subject of this book. This site is updated regularly. Please use this link to access the list: **www.powerkidslinks.com/iac/peop**